Heart H

Volume 1

Tony Thiessen

Kids discover how to memorize God's Word.

Off The Curb Publishing Co.
Escondido, Ca. 92026

Heart Hiders
Copyright © 1997 by Anthony S. Thiessen
All rights reserved. This book, or part thereof, may not be reproduced in any form without permission.

First edition: August 1997

Scripture taken from the New American Standard Bible ®,
Copyright © the Lockman Foundation 1960, 1962, 1963, 1968, 1971, 1972
1973, 1975, 1977, 1995 Used by permission

Scripture taken from The Holy Bible, New International Version (North American Edition), Copyright © 1973, 1978, 1984 by the International Bible Society. Used by permission of Zondervan Publishing House.

Scripture quotation marked NKJV are taken from the New King James Bible, copyright © 1979, 1980, 1982 by Thomas Nelson Inc. Used by permission. All rights reserved.

Scripture taken from the International Children's Bible, New Century Version, copyright © 1983, 1986, 1988 by Word Publishing, Dallas, Texas 75039. Used by permission.

ISBN 0-9660489-0-3
Printed in the United States of America

Off The Curb Publishing
306-N West El Norte Parkway Ste. 352
Escondido, Ca. 92026
(760)-738-7039   WWW.hearthiders.com

This book is dedicated to my children, Andy and Emily. May they grow to love God and His Word more each day.

Reward Stickers

The concept of <u>Heart</u> <u>Hiders</u> came to me one Sunday morning while sitting in church. Our pastor, Dennis Keating, was speaking about raising children. He said that several years ago his kids asked him what he wanted for Christmas. Not wanting another tie, he told them the best gift would be memorizing a passage of Scripture. What a great idea! This just happened to be two weeks before Mothers Day, so I began that afternoon on Psalm 23. By the time Mothers Day arrived, my four year old son Andy could recite the entire Psalm without looking at the paper! My wife was thrilled, as was I, so I set to work on the next verses. When our friends and family heard Andy recite, they all thought this should be made available to others. So began <u>Heart</u> <u>Hiders</u>.

As you can see, the verses are a combination of both words and pictures. These pictures are sometimes very clear in their meaning and at other times need to be deciphered. But in all cases, the words are printed after each verse.

I have used pictures for several reasons. First, my son Andy just turned four and has not yet learned to read. Second, the pictures help him (and me) to remember what comes next. This method of Scripture memory work, although designed for a child, can be very beneficial to people of all ages.

You may need to explain the pictures to young children because the concepts are new to them while older children will want minimal help as they try to figure out the meaning of a certain picture for themselves. This is a great way to spend time with your kids, not only memorizing God's Word, but also discussing the meaning of the verses. As you help your kids hide God's Word in their hearts, you will learn as well.

Children earn rewards for each verse they hide in their hearts. After a child memorizes and recites a verse, they can build "points" toward a personalized certificate of completion.

Keeping score is easy! Heart stickers are placed over the open Bible (starting on page 33) each time a verse is completed. This gives the child a sense of accomplishment and tracks the progress they are making.

Upon completion of all the verses, please send $3.00 shipping and handling to Heart Hiders 306-N West El Norte Pkwy. Escondido, CA 92026 to receive a personalized certificate of completion.

Enjoy this time of learning!

Table of Contents

Memorize God's Word

Psalm 119:11   1
Psalm 119:105   1
Proverbs 4:20-22   2
Proverbs 3:1-3   3
Proverbs 7:1-3   4

Salvation

John 3:16   5
2 Corinthians 5:17   6
John 1:12   6
Ephesians 2:8-10   7
Romans 6:23   8
John 14:6   8
Romans 3:23   9
Acts 4:12   9
Romans 10:9,10   10

Obedience

Colossians 3:20   11
Hebrews 13:17   12
Proverbs 1:8   13
Proverbs 13:1   13
Ephesians 6:1-3   14

Trust

Proverbs 3:5,6   15
Jeremiah 32:27   16
Psalm 37:4,5   16
Isaiah 41:10   17
Psalm 56:3   17
Philippians 4:13   18
Psalm 9:10   18

Assurance

1John 5:13	19
John 10:27,28	20
Romans 8:31	20
John 5:24	21
Psalm 118:6	21
Hebrews 13:8	22
Psalm 121:7,8	22

Love

1 John 4:18,19	23
1 Corinthians 13:4-8	24
John 15:13	25
1 Peter 4:8	26
1 Timothy 1:5	26
1 John 3:17,18	27
1 John 4:7,8	28
1 Corinthians 16:14	28

Forgiveness

1 John 1:9	29
Ephesians 4:32	30
Colossians 3:13	30
Romans 8:1	31
1 John 1:7	31

Memorize God's Word

Psalm 119:11

I have **hidden** your **word in** my **heart** that **I might not sin against you**.
NIV

Psalm 119:105

Your **word** is a **lamp to** my **feet** and a **light to** my **path**. NKJV

Proverbs 4:20-22

My **son, give attention to** my **words; incline** your **ear to** my **sayings**. Do **not** let them **depart** from your sight; keep them **in** the midst of your **heart**. **For** they **are life to** those **who** find them, and health **to** all their **whole body**. NASB

Proverbs 3:1-3

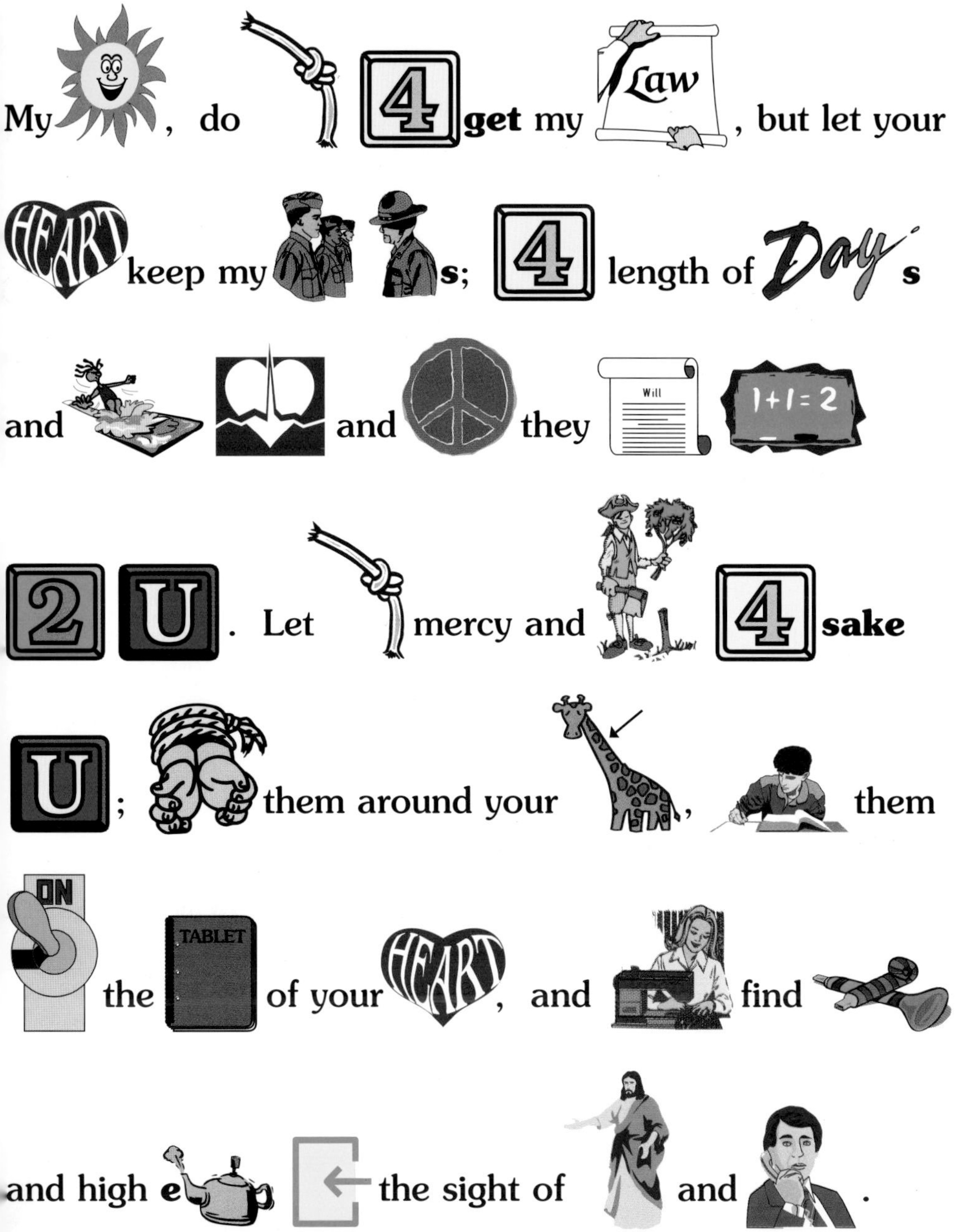
My , do get my Law , but let your
HEART keep my s; length of Day s
and and they Will 1+1=2
2 U . Let mercy and 4 sake
U ; them around your , them
ON the TABLET of your HEART , and find
and high e the sight of and .

My **son**, do **not forget** my **law**, but let your **heart** keep my **commands**; **for** length of **days** and **long life** and **peace** they **will add to you**. Let **not** mercy and **truth forsake you**; **bind** them around your **neck**, **write** them **on** the **tablet** of your **heart**, and **so** find **favor** and high **esteem in** the sight of **God** and **man**. NKJV

Proverbs 7:1-3

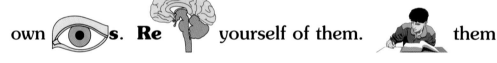

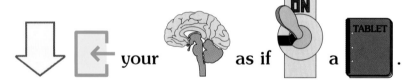

My **son, remember what I say**. **Treasure** my **commands**. **Obey** my **commands**, and **you will** live. Protect my **teachings** as **you would** your own **eyes**. **Remind** yourself of them. **Write** them **down in** your **mind** as if **on** a **tablet**. ICB

Salvation

John 3:16

For God so loved the **world** that He **gave His one** and only **Son**, that **whoever believes in** Him **shall not perish** but have **eternal life**. NIV

2 Corinthians 5:17

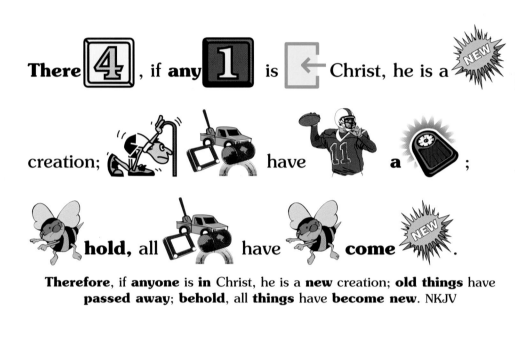

Therefore, if **anyone** is **in** Christ, he is a **new** creation; **old things** have **passed away**; **behold**, all **things** have **become new**. NKJV

John 1:12

But as many as **received** Him, **to** them He **gave** the right **to become** **children** of **God**, **to** those **who believe in His name**. NKJV

Ephesians 2:8-10

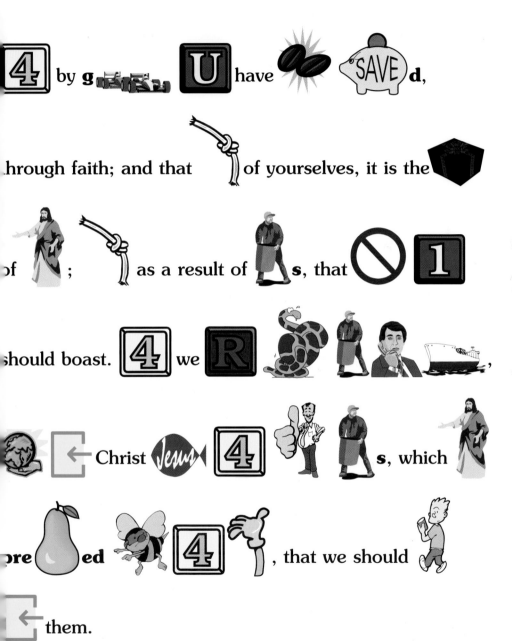

For by **grace you** have **been saved** through faith; and that **not** of yourselves, it is the **gift** of **God**; **not** as a result of **works**, that **no one** should boast. **For** we **are His workmanship**, **created in** Christ **Jesus for good works**, which **God prepared beforehand**, that we should **walk in** them.
NASB

Romans 6:23

LORD.

For the wages of **sin** is **death**, but the **gift** of **God** is **eternal life in** Christ **Jesus our** LORD. NKJV

John 14:6

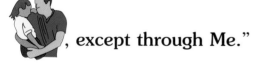, except through Me."

Jesus said **to** him, "**I am** the **way**, the **truth**, and the **life**. **No one** comes **to** the **Father** except through Me." NKJV

Romans 3:23

 all have  **ed** and  short of the of
 .

For all have **sinned** and **fall** short of the **glory** of **God**. NKJV

Acts 4:12

"And there is salvation   else;

there is other **Andy**  that has

 n among , by which we must

 **d**."

"And there is salvation **in no one** else; **for** there is **no** other **name under heaven** that has **been given** among **men**, by which we must **be saved**." NASB

Romans 10:9,10

If **you** use your **mouth to say**, "**Jesus** is LORD," and if **you believe in** your **heart** that **God raised Jesus** from **death**, then **you will be saved**. We **believe** with **our hearts**, and **so** we **are made** right with **God**. And we use **our mouths to say** that we **believe**, and **so** we **are saved**. ICB

Obedience

Colossians 3:20

Children, obey your **parents in** all **things, for** this is **well** pleasing **to** the LORD. NKJV

Hebrews 13:17

Obey those **who rule over you**, and **be submissive, for** they **watch out for** your **souls**, as those **who** must **give account**. Let them do **so** with joy and **not** with **grief, for** that **would be** unprofitable **for you**. NKJV

Proverbs 1:8

, my , your 's , and do

sake your 's .

Hear, my **son**, your **father's instruction**, and do **not forsake**
your **mother's teaching**. NASB

Proverbs 13:1

A heeds 's , but

a scoffer does  rebuke.

A **wise son** heeds **his father's instruction**, but a scoffer does
not listen to rebuke. **NKJV**

Ephesians 6:1-3

Children, obey your parents in the LORD, for this is right. "Honor your father and mother" - which is the first commandment with a promise - "that it may go well with you and that you may enjoy long life on the earth." NIV

Trust

Proverbs 3:5,6

Trust in the LORD with all your **heart,** and **lean not on** your own **understanding**; **in** all your **ways acknowledge** Him, and He **shall direct** your **paths**. NKJV

Jeremiah 32:27

" the LORD, the of all **kind**. Is anything hard Me?"

"**I am** the LORD, the **God** of all **mankind**. Is anything **too** hard **for** Me?" NIV

Psalm 37:4,5

De yourself the LORD; and He

 the desires of your . **Co** your

 the LORD, also Him, and He

 do it.

Delight yourself **in** the LORD; and He **will give you** the desires of your **heart**. **Commit** your **way to** the LORD, **trust also in** Him, and He **will** do it. NASB

Isaiah 41:10

So do **not fear, for I am** with **you**; do **not be dismayed, for I am** your
God. I will strengthen you and help **you; I will uphold you**
with my **righteous** right **hand.** NIV

Psalm 56:3

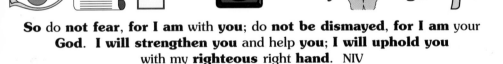

When **I am** afraid, **I will trust you.** ICB

Philippians 4:13

  do everything Him  s

me  .

I can do everything **through** Him **who gives** me **strength.** NIV

Psalm 9:10

And those  know Your **Andy**   their

   ;   , LORD, have

 saken those   .

And those **who** know Your **name will put** their **trust in You**; **for You**,
LORD, have **not forsaken** those **who seek You.** NKJV

Assurance

1 John 5:13

I write these things to you who believe in the name of the Son of God so that you may know that you have eternal life. NIV

John 10:27,28

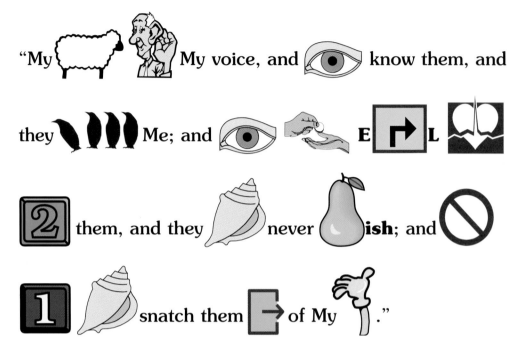

"My 🐑 👂 My voice, and 👁 know them, and they 🐧🐧🐧 Me; and 👁 ✋ E➡L ♥ 2️⃣ them, and they 🐚 never 🍐ish; and 🚫 1️⃣🐚 snatch them ➡ of My 🤚."

"My **sheep hear** My voice, and **I** know them, and they **follow** Me; and **I give eternal life to** them, and they **shall** never **perish**; and **no one shall** snatch them **out** of My **hand**." NASB

Romans 8:31

❓ then 🐚 we 📢 2️⃣ these 📻🚚 ? If 🧔 is 4️⃣ us, 🦉 🥤 🐝 👤 us?

What then **shall** we **say to** these **things**? If **God** is **for** us, **who can be against** us? NKJV

John 5:24

"I tell **you** the **truth**, **whoever hears** My **word** and **believes** Him **who sent** Me has **eternal life** and **will not be condemned**; He has **crossed over** from **death to life**." NIV

Psalm 118:6

The LORD is with me;   do me?

The LORD is with me; **I will not be** afraid. **What can man** do **to** me? NIV

Hebrews 13:8

 Christ is the same **yester**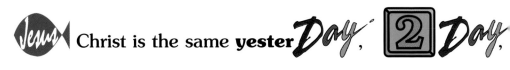

and **ever**.

Jesus Christ is the same **yesterday**, **today, and forever**. NKJV

Psalm 121:7,8

The LORD **shall preserve you** from all **evil**; He **shall preserve** your **soul**. The Lord **shall preserve** your **going out** and your coming **in** from this **time forth**, and **even forevermore**. NKJV

Love

1 John 4:18,19

There is **no fear in love**; but **perfect love casts out fear, because fear involves** torment. But he **who fears** has **not been made perfect in love**. We **love** Him **because** He **first loved** us. NKJV

1 Corinthians 13:4-8

 there **R** s, they cease;

there is knowledge, it vanish a .

Love suffers **long** and is kind; **love** does **not envy**; **love** does **not parade** itself, is **not** puffed **up**; does **not behave** rudely, does **not seek** its own, is **not** provoked, **thinks no evil**; does **not rejoice in** iniquity, but **rejoices in truth**; **bears** all **things**, **believes** all **things**, hopes all **things**, endures all **things**. **Love** never fails. But **whether** there **are** prophecies, they **will** fail; **whether** there **are tongues**, they **will** cease; **whether** there is knowledge, it **will** vanish **away**. NKJV

John 15:13

Greater **love** has **no one** than this, than **to lay down one's life for his friends**. NKJV

1 Peter 4:8

And above all **things** have fervent **love for one** another, **for love will** cover a multitude of **sins**. NKJV

1 Timothy 1:5

 **cere** faith.

The **goal** of this **command** is **love**, which comes from a **pure heart** and a **good conscience** and a **sincere** faith. NIV

1 John 3:17,18

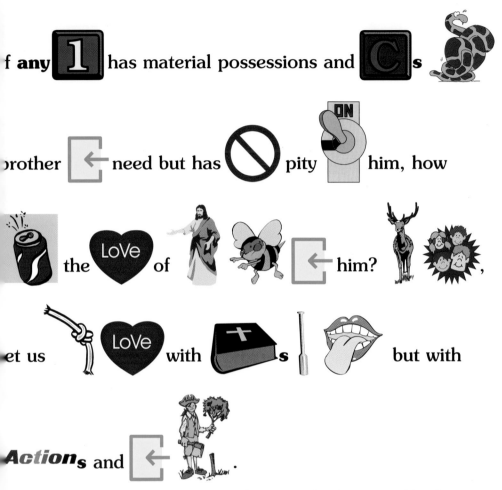

If **anyone** has material possessions and **sees his** brother **in** need but has **no** pity **on** him, how **can** the **love** of **God be in** him? **Dear children**, let us **not love** with **words or tongue** but with **actions** and **in truth**. NIV

1 John 4:7,8

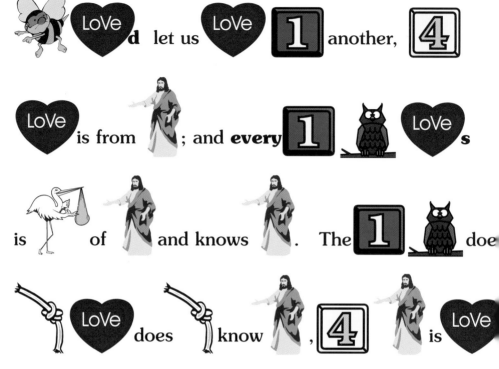

Beloved, let us **love one** another, **for love** is from **God**; and **everyone who loves** is **born** of **God** and knows **God**. The **one who** does **not love** does **not** know **God**, **for God** is **love**. NASB

1 Corinthians 16:14

Let all that **you** do **be** done with **love**. NKJV

Forgiveness

1 John 1:9

If we **confess our sins**, He is **faithful** and **just to forgive** us **our sins** and **to cleanse** us from all **unrighteousness**. NKJV

Ephesians 4:32

And 🐝 kind **2** **1** another, tender ❤ed,

4 🤲 **ing** each other, ⚖ as 🧎 ⬅

Christ also has **4** 🤲 n **U**.

And **be** kind **to one** another, **tenderhearted**, **forgiving** each other, **just** as **God in** Christ also has **forgiven you**. NASB

Colossians 3:13

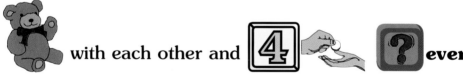

🧸 with each other and **4** 🤲 **?** ever

grievances **U** M🌼y have 🧍 **1** another.

4 🤲 as the LORD **4** 🗳 **U**.

Bear with each other and **forgive whatever** grievances **you may** have **against one** another. **Forgive** as the LORD **forgave you**. NIV

Romans 8:1

There is **therefore** now **no condemnation for** those **who
are in** Christ **Jesus**. NASB

1 John 1:7

But if we **walk in** the **light** as He Himself is **in** the **light**, we have
fellowship with **one** another, and the **blood** of **Jesus His Son**
cleanses us from all **sin**. NASB

"I Did It!"

After memorizing a verse, put a heart sticker over the open Bible to show which ones you've done. When all the verses have been memorized, send $3.00 shipping and handling to Heart Hiders 306-N West El Norte Parkway Ste. 352 Escondido, Ca. 92026 to receive your personalized certificate of completion.

Each time you're ready to place a new sticker, go back to the verses you've already hidden in your heart and recite them again. This will help keep God's Word in your heart and mind.

Memorize God's Word

 Psalm 119:11

 Psalm 119:105

 Proverbs 4:20-22

 Proverbs 3:1-3

 Proverbs 7:1-3

Salvation

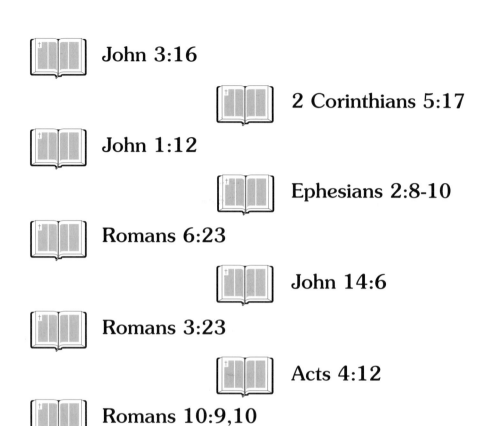

John 3:16

2 Corinthians 5:17

John 1:12

Ephesians 2:8-10

Romans 6:23

John 14:6

Romans 3:23

Acts 4:12

Romans 10:9,10

Obedience

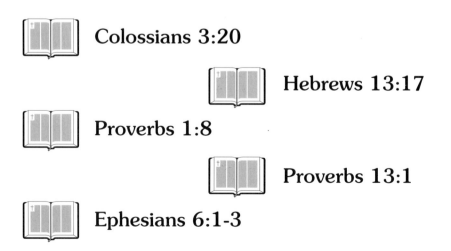

Colossians 3:20

Hebrews 13:17

Proverbs 1:8

Proverbs 13:1

Ephesians 6:1-3

Trust

 Proverbs 3:5,6

 Jeremiah 32:27

 Psalm 37:4,5

 Isaiah 41:10

 Psalm 56:3

 Philippians 4:13

 Psalm 9:10

Assurance

 1John 5:13

 John 10:27,28

 Romans 8:31

 John 5:24

 Psalm 118:6

 Hebrews 13:8

 Psalm 121:7,8

Love

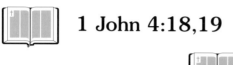 1 John 4:18,19

 1 Corinthians 13:4-8

 John 15:13

 1 Peter 4:8

 1 Timothy 1:5

 1 John 3:17,18

 1 John 4:7,8

 1 Corinthians 16:14

Forgiveness

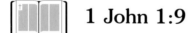 1 John 1:9

 Ephesians 4:32

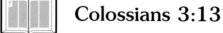 Colossians 3:13

 Romans 8:1

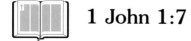 1 John 1:7

Great News!
I Have Hidden God's Word In My Heart!

_____ has memorized all of
the verses in Heart Hiders Volume 1. The date of
completion was _____.

Please send a Heart Hiders bookmark and a
personalized certificate of completion to:

Please Print
Name_____ Phone (___) _____
Address_____
City_____ State_____ Zip _____

Please send to:
Off The Curb Publications
306-N West El Norte Parkway Ste. 352
Escondido, Ca. 92026

Did You Borrow This Book? Want A Copy Of Your Own?

Need A Gift For A Friend or Loved One?

ORDER FORM

YES! I would like to help my children hide God's Word in their hearts. Please send _____ copies of Heart Hiders Volume 1. I have enclosed $9.95 per copy + $3.00 S & H for first book, $1.00 for each additional book.

California residents include $0.80 state sales tax per book. (Canadian orders must be accompanied by a postal money order in U.S. funds.) Allow 2 weeks for delivery.

Check enclosed for $_____ (payable to Off the Curb Publishing)
Charge my _____ Mastercard _____ Visa
Account No._____ Exp. Date_____
Signature_____

Name _____ Phone (___)_____
Address_____
City_____ State_____ Zip_____

Off the Curb Publishing
306-N West El Norte Parkway Suite 352
Escondido, CA 92026
(760)738-7039 Fax (760)738-6038

For more information about Off The Curb Publishing, other products or to place an electronic order, check out our web site at WWW.hearthiders.com.

QUANTITY ORDERS INVITED
For bulk discount prices, please call (760) 738-7039